IN THE
NATIONAL INTEREST

General Sir John Monash once exhorted a graduating class to 'equip yourself for life, not solely for your own benefit but for the benefit of the whole community'. At the university established in his name, we repeat this statement to our own graduating classes, to acknowledge how important it is that common or public good flows from education.

Universities spread and build on the knowledge they acquire through scholarship in many ways, well beyond the transmission of this learning through education. It is a necessary part of a university's role to debate its findings, not only with other researchers and scholars, but also with the broader community in which it resides.

Publishing for the benefit of society is an important part of a university's commitment to free intellectual inquiry. A university provides civil space for such inquiry by its scholars, as well as for investigations by public intellectuals and expert practitioners.

This series, In the National Interest, embodies Monash University's mission to extend knowledge and encourage informed debate about matters of great significance to Australia's future.

Professor Susan Elliott AM
Interim President and Vice-Chancellor,
Monash University

RONLI SIFRIS
TOWARDS REPRODUCTIVE JUSTICE

MONASH
UNIVERSITY
PUBLISHING

Monash University Publishing
Matheson Library Annexe
40 Exhibition Walk
Monash University
Clayton, Victoria 3800, Australia
https://publishing.monash.edu

Monash University Publishing brings to the world publications which advance the best traditions of humane and enlightened thought.

ISBN: 9781922979469 (paperback)
ISBN: 9781922979483 (ebook)

Series: In the National Interest
Editor: Greg Bain
Project manager & copyeditor: Paul Smitz
Designer: Peter Long
Typesetter: Cannon Typesetting
Proofreader: Gillian Armitage
Printed in Australia by Ligare Book Printers

A catalogue record for this book is available from the National Library of Australia.

This book is dedicated to my daughter, Eden Mia Sifris Ross. With her innate sense of fairness and compassion, I have no doubt she will grow up to be a warrior for justice.

TOWARDS REPRODUCTIVE JUSTICE

In 1973, the Supreme Court of the United States handed down its famous decision of *Roe v Wade*, declaring abortion a constitutionally protected right located within the right to privacy in the United States Bill of Rights. Fast-forward to June 2022, almost fifty years after this landmark case, and the US Supreme Court handed down another decision whose impact reverberated around the world. The case was *Dobbs v Jackson Women's Health Organization* and it concerned a Mississippi law that banned abortions after fifteen weeks' gestation. The Jackson Women's Health Organization, a Mississippi abortion clinic, had challenged the law as constitutionally invalid. But the Supreme Court upheld the law, and in doing so overturned *Roe v Wade*, removing the constitutional protection for abortion.

The immediate impact of this decision was that abortion regulation reverted to the American states.

Each state could decide for itself whether to enact legal restrictions on access to abortion. In anticipation of this decision, several states had already passed so-called 'trigger laws', which became enlivened as soon as *Roe v Wade* was overturned, while others were quick to enact restrictive regulation. At the time of writing, a number of US states were enforcing an almost-complete ban on abortion, with very limited exceptions. These include Texas, Missouri, Idaho, North Dakota, South Dakota, Arkansas, Oklahoma, Louisiana, Indiana, West Virginia, Kentucky, Tennessee, Mississippi, Alabama and South Carolina.

The impact on people seeking to terminate a pregnancy in the states that restrict abortion access has been devastating. Predictably, these restrictions have disproportionately affected the poorest and most vulnerable people, those who are unable to travel to more liberal states to access abortion services. The story of abortion in the United States has become a tale of two countries—there are those states, predominantly in the Deep South and Midwest, where abortion access is either severely restricted or banned altogether, and then there are the other states with liberal access laws, which have become destinations for desperate people travelling in search of a lawful abortion.[1]

The overturning of *Roe v Wade* prompted pro-choice protests and rallies in numerous countries, including Australia. While the Australian legal, social and political contexts are very different to those of the United States, the notion that abortion could be legal one day and completely banned the next gave Australians cause to consider the extent to which reproductive rights are protected, and reproductive health care is accessible, here at home. And so it should.

To contemplate such questions, it is necessary to first frame the right to terminate a pregnancy as a human rights issue, noting that the international human rights regime has been increasingly critical of restrictions on access to abortion and has progressively advocated for countries to take active steps to facilitate access. We can then consider the Australian laws and policies that have advanced reproductive rights. These include the wave of decriminalisation that has swept across Australia, legal measures to mitigate the impact of conscientious objection, and the introduction of safe access zones around abortion clinics. At the same time, the enduring barriers to abortion access in Australia need to be illuminated, so we can acknowledge the remaining steps on the path to achieving full reproductive justice. Among these are the attitudes of some health professionals and health facilities, financial and geographic barriers, deficiencies in medical training, and persisting legal obstacles. It is also worth examining recent relevant legal and policy developments—both those that contribute to the advancement of reproductive rights in Australia, and those that detract from this crucial goal. It should also be noted that, throughout this book, in approaching the issue from an inclusive feminist perspective, I have endeavoured where possible to use gender-neutral language.

REPRODUCTIVE RIGHTS ARE HUMAN RIGHTS

Abortion access is a human rights issue. This is relevant not only from a theoretical perspective, in that Australia views itself, and represents itself, as a rights-respecting society, but also from a practical perspective. For example, rights have pragmatic value because they provide the authority to support movements for social change. This is not to say that countries change their approach to abortion merely because the international human rights regime calls for such a change (although they may do so), but rather that human rights have been, and continue to be, an important part of the toolkit used by activists and advocates in the fight for reproductive justice. Governments have a responsibility to ensure that people's fundamental rights are adequately protected, and they may be shamed on the world stage if they fail to fulfil this duty.

In recent years, the call for full decriminalisation of abortion has grown louder around the world, with the international human rights regime increasingly seeking the *complete* decriminalisation of abortion rather than decriminalisation on specific grounds, such as where the health or life of the pregnant person is endangered. One of the reasons why the full decriminalisation of abortion is important is because abortion cannot be a right if it is a crime. It would be inconsistent (and incoherent) for a country to accept that a pregnant person has a right to access abortion services and at the same time to criminalise access to those very services. So the significance of recognising abortion as a human rights issue goes hand in hand with accepting that it cannot be a crime. This is one reason why the decriminalisation of abortion in Australia is noteworthy, as I discuss later in this book.

Further, the international human rights regime has thankfully moved beyond the neoliberal approach of merely requiring that countries refrain from negatively interfering with access to abortion, such as through restrictive abortion legislation. Rather, international human rights law also imposes a positive duty requiring countries to be proactive in ensuring the availability and accessibility of quality abortion services. Such an approach recognises that having 'good laws' is important, but this is not sufficient in itself to secure access. The fulfilment of reproductive rights requires more than just laws that do not infringe human rights.

Australia represents itself as a rights-respecting society even though it does not have a federal constitutional Bill of rights, and it is the only Western liberal democracy without even a legislative Bill of rights—although this may change given that the Parliamentary Joint Committee on Human Rights is currently conducting an inquiry into Australia's human rights framework. Nevertheless, in line with its professed status as a country that cares about human rights, Australia has ratified the key international human rights treaties, including the *International Covenant on Civil and Political Rights* and the *International Covenant on Economic, Social and Cultural Rights*, which, together with the *Universal Declaration of Human Rights*, are often referred to as the International Bill of Human Rights.

Australia has also ratified (among other conventions) the *Convention against Torture and Other Cruel, Inhuman or Degrading Treatment or Punishment*; the *Convention on the Elimination of All Forms of Discrimination against Women*; and the *Convention on the Rights of the Child*. These conventions are multilateral treaties that have been ratified by over 150 countries, and they form the bedrock of the international human rights system. Ratification is a statement to the world that a country binds itself under international law to the terms of that treaty, as Australia has done. And the treaty bodies administering each of these conventions have made it clear that they view access to abortion as a human right. This has been communicated by, for example, decisions made in response to individual complaints, general comments or recommendations setting out how provisions should be interpreted, and concluding observations relating to the conduct of individual countries.

While international human rights law does not enshrine a right to abortion per se, it has been viewed as falling within a number of existing, clearly recognised human rights. Restricting access to safe and legal abortion services may be seen as constituting a violation of the right to life, right to health, right to privacy, right to equality / freedom from discrimination, and right to be free from torture or cruel, inhuman or degrading treatment or punishment.

These rights are of course interdependent, and the same conduct may violate multiple rights. A legal restriction on access to abortion that leads a pregnant person to undergo a clandestine, unsafe abortion may violate that person's right to health, privacy and equality, as well as their right to be free from inhuman and degrading treatment—all at the same time. So it is somewhat artificial to analyse each right individually. However, for the sake of clarity, and to illustrate the extent to which barriers to abortion access interact with each of these rights, I will discuss the relevant rights separately.

The Right to Life and Health

Access to safe and lawful abortion services is crucial to protecting the right to life of the pregnant person. According to the World Health Organization (WHO), each year, 4.7–13.2 per cent of maternal deaths worldwide are attributable to unsafe abortions.[2] It is clear from the evidence that banning abortion does not actually prevent abortions from occurring, as desperate people will take desperate measures.

Those who cannot access abortion lawfully may resort to unsafe, so-called 'backyard abortions'.

The United Nations (UN) Human Rights Committee has raised the issue of unsafe abortions in the context of the right to life, as part of its role in interpreting the *International Covenant on Civil and Political Rights*. The committee has referred to 'life-threatening clandestine abortions' in its General Comment No. 28. More recently, in its General Comment No. 36, which focused specifically on the right to life, the committee noted that restrictions on abortion must not jeopardise the lives of pregnant people, and by extension that countries have a positive duty to provide 'safe, legal and effective access to abortion'.

Both the WHO and the Human Rights Committee have recognised that unsafe abortions jeopardise the right to life of the pregnant person. Whereas death as a consequence of an unsafe abortion is clearly the extreme scenario, even where an unsafe abortion does not result in death, it may still have a significant negative impact on the person's right to health. This is a statement of the obvious. If a medical procedure is performed in a context where traditional safety protocols are not adhered to, then of course there is an increase in the potential for harm to health, as against a scenario where there is compliance with safety protocols. Imagine for a moment that appendectomies are illegal in certain contexts, and that people needing them have to resort to clandestine procedures in the back room of someone's home, rather than in a sterile hospital environment. The risk of infection and other health complications would inarguably be higher.

Further, in addition to the risks inherent in performing an unsafe abortion, forcing a person to continue with a pregnancy may pose its own risks. This is the reason why, even before abortion was decriminalised in Australia, the law had carved out an exception to the crime of abortion in circumstances where the pregnancy posed a risk to the person's health. It is also one of the reasons why, in Australia today, a pregnant person who is no longer able to access abortion 'on request' may still legally terminate a pregnancy. For example, in Victoria, abortion 'on request' is legally available until twenty-four weeks' gestation, and beyond that point it is available where two doctors agree it is appropriate in the circumstances. This could entail considerations relating to the person's health and wellbeing.

Back in 1994, the international community was already recognising access to safe abortion as a healthcare matter. The UN-published report of the International Conference on Population and

Development, which took place in Cairo, urged countries to strengthen their commitment to women's health by addressing the major public health concern posed by unsafe abortion. More recently, in May 2016, the UN Committee on Economic, Social and Cultural Rights, which is responsible for monitoring the implementation of the *International Covenant on Economic, Social and Cultural Rights*, released its General Comment No. 22, which focused on the right to sexual and reproductive health. In this comment, the committee recognised that the 'right to sexual and reproductive health is an integral part of the right to health enshrined in article 12 of the *International Covenant on Economic, Social and Cultural Rights*', and it explicitly included the right to elective abortion as falling within the right to reproductive health. It also expressed the view that it is not enough for countries to liberalise their laws. They need to proactively secure access to the full range of reproductive healthcare services.

In the June 2023 decision of *Camila v Peru*, the UN Committee on the Rights of the Child, which is responsible for monitoring the implementation of the *Convention on the Rights of the Child*, found Peru to be in violation of the rights to health and life of a rural indigenous teenager who became pregnant as a result of being raped by her father. A hospital attended by the teenager refused to terminate the pregnancy, despite therapeutic abortion being legal in Peru. The committee found that, in these circumstances, Peru's failure to provide Camila with access to abortion services exposed her to serious risk. This was exacerbated by the fact that, after miscarrying, she was prosecuted for 'self-abortion'. That said, in August 2023, following pressure from the UN, an eleven-year-old rape victim was provided with abortion services after initially being refused access. This suggests that Peru is feeling the weight of the insistence of the international human rights community that abortion access be facilitated in such circumstances. It illustrates the capacity of international human rights law to propel change, despite the lack of concrete enforcement measures.

In the past, pro-choice activists focused on fighting for decriminalisation and for countries to refrain from legally restricting abortion access. However, the past fifty years have been characterised by a global trend towards the liberalisation of abortion laws. As a result, the pro-choice community, alongside the international human rights regime, has become more ambitious in its aspirations. It does not simply seek non-interference by those in power, but the active facilitation of access to abortion. Accordingly, we are seeing the gradual emergence of a willingness to acknowledge the importance of securing access to safe and legal abortion services as a core component of the broader right to health. Decriminalisation of abortion alone is insufficient. The right to health requires the provision of access to services *in addition to* the removal of impediments to access.

The Right to Privacy

As I mentioned earlier, when the US Supreme Court decided *Roe v Wade* back in 1973, it located the right to abortion within the right to privacy in the US Constitution. It is relevant to note that the right to privacy is frequently used interchangeably with the right to autonomy, as it is regarded as a right to personal or individual liberty. The right to autonomy is one of the key bioethical principles underpinning many aspects of health law in countries like Australia. For example, the legal concept of informed consent is based on the notion that an individual has the right to make an informed decision regarding whether to accept or refuse medical treatment.

The UN Human Rights Committee has handed down several decisions locating the right to abortion within the right to privacy found in article 17 of the *International Covenant on Civil and Political Rights*. In the decisions of *Llantoy Huamán v Peru* and *LMR v Argentina*, the committee formed the view that both the right to privacy and the right to be free from torture and ill-treatment were infringed by the failure of the countries involved to ensure that vulnerable complainants were able to access lawful abortion services. In the more recent decisions of *Mellet v Ireland* and *Whelan v Ireland*, the committee also found a violation of the right to be free from discrimination (in addition to the right to privacy and right to be free from torture and ill-treatment). While these decisions are not binding in the same way as a decision of, say, a domestic court, they represent an authoritative interpretation of the treaty. As such, there is an expectation that the country which is the subject of the complaint will take steps to implement the committee's recommendations. The decision also acts as a statement to other countries that have ratified the treaty (known as states parties) of the committee's understanding of the rights and corresponding duties enshrined in the treaty.

The landmark 2005 decision of *Llantoy Huamán v Peru* involved a seventeen-year-old Peruvian who was raped and became pregnant with what a scan showed to be an anencephalic foetus. Anencephaly is a condition incompatible with life, meaning that if the teenager was forced to continue the pregnancy to term, the consequence of this would be to give birth to a baby who would not survive beyond a few days. Despite her expressed desire to terminate the pregnancy, the hospital refused, claiming it would be illegal in such circumstances. This reasoning was questionable, as the Peruvian *Criminal Code* provides a limited exception to the crime of abortion in cases of therapeutic abortion. As predicted, the teenager gave birth to an anencephalic baby who survived for four days and, following the baby's death, she fell into a state of deep depression. The Human Rights Committee formed the view that she suffered severe psychological harm as a result of being compelled to continue with her pregnancy. It found Peru to be in breach of the article 17 right to privacy, as well as other rights.

In 2011, in *LMR v Argentina*, the Human Rights Committee decided another relevant complaint, this time involving a woman with an intellectual disability who became pregnant as a result of rape. Argentina's failure to provide access to abortion services led her to terminate the pregnancy via an illegal abortion, putting her life and health at risk. The committee decided that Argentina's failure to guarantee this woman the right to terminate her pregnancy constituted a violation of her article 17 right to privacy, as well as a violation of other rights such as the article 7 right to be free from torture and ill-treatment. Illustrating the impact of international human rights norms on the domestic realm,

> the case added to a growing normative consensus under international law regarding the need to ensure access to therapeutic abortion in practice; it also broadened the debate within Argentine society and government sectors because it had become a matter of compliance with international human rights.[3]

In December 2020, abortion was legalised in Argentina. Accordingly, in the decisions of *Llantoy Huamán v Peru* and *LMR v Argentina*, the Human Rights Committee formed the view that both the right to privacy and the right to be free from torture and ill-treatment were infringed by the failure of the countries involved to ensure that these vulnerable complainants were able to access lawful abortion services.

It is not only South American countries that have been rebuked by the Human Rights Committee for failing to provide access to abortion services. In 2016 and 2017, the committee handed down two decisions against Ireland involving similar factual scenarios. *Mellet v Ireland* involved a woman who, when twenty-one weeks' pregnant, was informed that her foetus had congenital abnormalities incompatible with life. At the time, abortion was prohibited under Irish law except where there was a real and substantial risk to the pregnant person's life. In fact, the Irish Constitution had enshrined the 'right to life of the unborn' in its Eighth Amendment. As a result, Amanda Mellet travelled to Liverpool in England to terminate her pregnancy. One can only imagine how stressful it would be to have to deal with such a foetal diagnosis, let alone the added trauma of having to travel to another country to access a lawful abortion. As in the preceding cases, the Human Rights Committee found that Ireland had violated Amanda's right to privacy, as well as her right to be free from torture and ill-treatment. In this case, the committee also found a violation of the right to be free from discrimination.

Whelan v Ireland was a 2017 decision involving a woman who was similarly informed, when twenty weeks' pregnant, that her foetus was likely to die in utero or shortly after birth. She, too, travelled internationally to terminate the pregnancy as a result of Ireland's legal prohibition on abortion. In line with its earlier decision in *Mellet v Ireland*, the Human Rights Committee decided that Ireland had violated the article 7 right to be free from torture, the article 17 right to privacy and the article 26 right to be free from discrimination.

It is interesting to note that in May 2018, a referendum was held to repeal the Eighth Amendment to the Irish Constitution. This referendum was successful, following which abortion was legalised and regulated in certain defined circumstances. I raise this to make the point, firstly, that the law in Ireland has changed since the above complaints were heard, and secondly, because this is a useful example of the potential of the international human rights regime to contribute to efforts to bring about change. There were no doubt other factors and influences that led the Irish people to change their law, but the pressure from the international human rights system served as an additional (and important) string in the bow of pro-choice activists and advocates.

The Right to Equality / Freedom from Discrimination

When the US Supreme Court handed down its decision of *Roe v Wade*, locating the right to abortion within the right to privacy in the American Constitution, many feminists were critical on the basis that the right to equality was just as relevant as the right to privacy, if not more so. Renowned feminist jurist Ruth Bader Ginsburg maintained that restrictions on abortion violate both the right to autonomy and the principle of equality, and criticised *Roe v Wade* on the ground that it focused on the former to the exclusion of the latter. She famously commented that '[i]t is essential to woman's equality with man that she be the decision maker, that her choice be controlling'.[4] North American scholars such as Reva Siegel have persuasively argued that one of the hallmarks of patriarchy is the restriction of women's autonomy, highlighting the connection between violations of women's autonomy and discrimination against women.[5]

Further, the right to privacy has for centuries been invoked as a justification for the refusal of the state (in the sense of the nation-state) to interfere in matters of 'private violence' against women. To understand the prevalence of state refusal to adequately address those forms of gender-based violence that occur within the home, one need look no further than the fact that the recognition of domestic violence as 'real violence' is a relatively recent phenomenon. This reality reinforces the need to explode the private into the public sphere and to tear down illusory boundaries.[6] The personal is political, and it should not be possible for countries to hide behind 'privacy' to justify turning a blind eye to harms that are perpetrated in the private sphere.

The international human rights regime is increasingly viewing the issue of abortion through the lens of equality. In its General Comment No. 14, when discussing the elimination of discrimination against women, the UN Committee on Economic, Social and Cultural Rights stressed the importance of providing access to high-quality, affordable sexual and reproductive services, as well as the removal of barriers interfering with access to sexual and reproductive health. Further, in its 1999 General Recommendation No. 24 on women and health, the UN Committee on the Elimination of Discrimination against Women (responsible for monitoring the implementation of the *Convention on the Elimination of All Forms of Discrimination against Women*) stated that '[i]t is discriminatory for a State party to refuse to provide legally for the performance of certain reproductive health services for women'. More recently, in 2017, this committee adopted General Recommendation No. 35, which viewed discriminatory legal provisions, including the criminalisation of abortion, as a form of gender-based violence, and clearly articulated that gender-based violence encompasses the forced continuation of pregnancy.

Notably, in October 2011, the Committee on the Elimination of Discrimination against Women handed down a decision concluding that, in certain circumstances, restricting access to abortion may constitute discrimination. The case of *LC v Peru* involved a teenage victim of sexual abuse who became pregnant as a result of that abuse. She survived a suicide attempt but sustained serious injuries. The hospital decided that emergency surgery posed a risk to the pregnancy and refused to provide the surgery, or to terminate the pregnancy—even though it clearly posed a danger to LC's physical and mental health, and therapeutic abortion was legal in Peru. In doing this, the hospital adopted a similar approach to that which was the subject of condemnation by the Human Rights Committee in the 2005 decision of *Llantoy Huamán v Peru* discussed earlier. The committee held that the hospital's refusal to terminate the pregnancy and to perform the necessary surgery in a time effective manner constituted a violation of the *Convention on the Elimination of All Forms of Discrimination against Women*.

In addition, as discussed above, the Human Rights Committee also found restrictions on abortion access constituted a violation of the right to be free from discrimination in the cases of *Mellet v Ireland* and

Whelan v Ireland. So it seems that the adoption of a discrimination/equality-based approach to conceptualising access to abortion is gaining momentum at the international level.

The Right to Be Free from Torture and Other Cruel, Inhuman or Degrading Treatment

In my book *Reproductive Freedom, Torture and International Human Rights: Challenging the Masculinisation of Torture* (2014), I provided a detailed argument for why restrictions on access to abortion may, in certain circumstances, constitute torture or other cruel, inhuman or degrading treatment. I framed my argument through a feminist lens, explaining how—like domestic legal systems—international law, too, was developed by men for men. So traditional understandings of torture and other cruel, inhuman or degrading treatment were focused on the forms of conduct to which men were disproportionately subjected, such as the methods sometimes used to elicit information from political prisoners. They neglected to consider those forms of conduct to which women were disproportionately subjected. Feminist scholars, however, were agitating for a change of approach, specifically for conduct like rape and domestic violence to be categorised as torture in circumstances where the conduct reaches that threshold, and where responsibility can be attributed to the state. My book added to this feminist argument.

The right to be free from torture and other cruel, inhuman or degrading treatment can be found in article 7 of the *International Covenant on Civil and Political Rights*, the treaty administered by the Human Rights Committee. Of particular relevance here is the committee's aforementioned landmark decision of *Llantoy Huamán v Peru*, in which it decided that Peru's failure to provide abortion services to a seventeen-year-old pregnant with an anencephalic foetus violated article 7. Similarly, in *LMR v Argentina*, the committee found Argentina to be in breach of article 7 when it failed to provide a mentally impaired rape victim with access to abortion. And such views were once again expressed in the decisions *Mellet v Ireland* and *Whelan v Ireland*.

The Human Rights Committee has also used its general comments and concluding observations to advance the view that certain forms of conduct that disproportionately affect women may constitute a violation of article 7. For example, in its General Comment No. 28 on equality of rights between men and women, the committee indicated that the article 7 right to be free from torture and ill-treatment may be violated in circumstances where responsibility can be attributed to a state for domestic violence, rape, certain restrictions on abortion, forced sterilisation, forced abortion or genital mutilation. In addition, concluding observations on various countries have been used to express the view that the criminalisation of abortion and the prevalence of unsafe abortions may also constitute a violation of article 7.

The key international treaty in this context is the *Convention against Torture and Other Cruel, Inhuman or Degrading Treatment or Punishment*. Like the Human Rights Committee, the committee administering the *Convention against Torture* has also adopted an increasingly expansive approach to the prohibition of torture and ill-treatment, particularly with regard to gender-based concerns. For example, in its General Comment No. 2, this committee pointed out that a state's responsibility includes a duty to exercise due diligence with respect to the conduct of private actors, and it had 'applied this principle to States parties' failure to prevent and protect victims from gender-based violence, such as rape, domestic violence, female genital mutilation, and trafficking'. The committee also emphasised the need to protect vulnerable or marginalised groups, and highlighted the significance of gender in this context, noting the relevance of medical treatment involving reproductive decisions.

Similarly, in its concluding observations, the committee has raised abortion access as a relevant concern. It has found that complete bans on abortion may constitute torture or ill-treatment and recommended that abortion be legal where a pregnancy would cause severe physical or mental suffering, such as where the pregnant person's health or life was at risk, where they were the victim of sexual violence, or when carrying a non-viable foetus. The committee has also expressed the view that denying a person access to abortion where it is lawful may violate the convention.

Unfortunately, this committee has not heard a complaint specifically addressing the issue of abortion access. That said, in several decisions it has interpreted conduct constituting torture or ill-treatment as stretching beyond the traditional male-centric paradigm. For example, in *VL v Switzerland* the committee found that sexual abuse by the police constituted torture despite being perpetrated outside of the formal detention facilities. The acceptance by the committee, in various contexts, that the conduct of private actors may be brought home to the state and may therefore constitute torture or ill-treatment is also evidence of the shift towards a less male-centric conception of torture.

Former UN special rapporteur Manfred Nowak dedicated an entire section of a landmark 2008 report to a discussion of 'a gender-sensitive interpretation of torture', considering the ways in which certain forms of behaviour that disproportionately affect women may constitute torture or ill-treatment.[7] As part of this discussion, Nowak focused on rape and sexual violence, violence against pregnant people, and the denial of reproductive rights, as well as violence in the private sphere such as intimate partner violence and female genital mutilation. Subsequent special rapporteurs, of this mandate and others, have clearly expressed the view that denial of abortion services may violate the prohibition of torture and ill-treatment.

Next Steps

The international human rights regime has recognised the right to terminate a pregnancy as falling within the existing international human rights paradigm. Experts in this field have observed that

> UN treaty monitoring bodies ... have clearly established that when abortion is legal under

domestic law, it must be accessible in practice, and that denials of access to legal abortion services can amount to violations of the rights to health, privacy, non-discrimination, and freedom from cruel, inhuman, and degrading treatment.[8]

They have further observed that, recently, 'these bodies have moved beyond articulating the specific grounds under which abortion should be legal and have urged states to generally ensure women's access to safe abortion services in connection with states' obligation to guarantee comprehensive reproductive health services'.[9]

Unfortunately, to date, the relevant treaty body decisions have been limited to especially extreme and tragic factual scenarios, such as those discussed earlier involving young rape victims and circumstances of foetal abnormality deemed incompatible with life. I would like to see a treaty body decide a case that is not an especially tragic case, and decide that case in favour of the complainant. In other words, I would like a complaint to come before the Committee on the Elimination of Discrimination against Women or the Human Rights Committee that is more akin to the circumstances in which most Australians seeking an abortion tend to find themselves; for example, a person complaining they were not provided with access to abortion services in circumstances where they were seeking an early gestation abortion for undisclosed reasons—not because there was a traumatic diagnosis of foetal abnormality or a shocking conception story. And I would like to see one of the UN committees decide that, in these fairly nondescript circumstances, a failure to provide access to abortion violates human rights norms. Such a decision would foreground the rights of the pregnant person and constitute a clear statement that abortion, regardless of the surrounding circumstances, is a matter of personal choice. This decision would clearly recognise that the choice to terminate any pregnancy is a matter of individual autonomy, and an essential precursor to equality.

Having positioned abortion within the international human rights framework, what about abortion in Australia? How is it regulated and how available is it? Is Australia complying with its international human rights obligations to provide access to the full range of reproductive healthcare services?

ABORTION LAW IN AUSTRALIA

Australia is a federation, meaning that some subject areas are regulated at the federal level and some are regulated at the state or territory level. Pursuant to the Australian Constitution, some matters are exclusively regulated by the Commonwealth, others are wholly the subject of state regulation, and there are some matters over which both state and federal parliaments have regulatory power. Abortion is, for the most part, regulated at the state and territory level. This is similar to many other areas of health law; for example, assisted reproductive treatment is also regulated at the state level, as is voluntary assisted dying.

One of the concerns with regulating issues like abortion at the state level is that there are invariably differences between the regulatory approaches of the different jurisdictions. This can result in what has been called 'reproductive tourism', as has been seen in the abortion context—when the laws of some jurisdictions provide for easier access to a healthcare service than others, the consequence is that people in need will travel to secure access. It can also exacerbate the impact of socio-economic differences, as those who are more privileged may be able to travel to access health care, whereas the more marginalised and vulnerable members of society may be unable to do so. This has become abundantly clear in the United States since the overturning of *Roe v Wade*, where people living in states with restrictive abortion laws now need to travel to more liberal states to access abortion. The impact is felt most acutely by those who are most vulnerable, and who are unable to travel: people who cannot leave their children to travel to another state; people who do not have the financial means to travel; or victims of domestic violence who cannot easily escape to another jurisdiction, even for a few days. However, in recent years there has been a move towards greater uniformity between Australian jurisdictions, beginning with the nationwide wave of decriminalisation.

In the early days of the white colonial settlement of the Australian continent, abortion law followed the British 1861 *Offences Against the Person Act*, sections 58 and 59 of which criminalised abortion. In the 1960s, the liberalisation of abortion laws began in the form of legislative reform and court rulings in cases where doctors were prosecuted, such as the 1969 decision of the Supreme Court of Victoria in *R v Davidson*. The case involved the prosecution of Dr Charles Davidson for performing an unlawful abortion. Justice Menhennitt invoked the common law principle of necessity to conclude that abortion was lawful where a doctor honestly believed it was necessary to protect the pregnant person from serious danger to life or health, and that it was a proportionate response to such danger. This exception to the crime of abortion became known as the 'Menhennitt Rules' and formed the law relating to abortion in Victoria until legislative reform took place in 2008.

In 2002, the Australian Capital Territory led the way in decriminalising abortion, and since then all remaining jurisdictions have followed suit, with the most recent being Western Australia in September 2023. The decriminalisation of abortion is noteworthy, despite the fact that even when criminalised, abortion was still widely legally available due to exceptions to the criminal law that had developed through the common law (being judge-made law) or via legislation, depending on the jurisdiction.

Victoria is one jurisdiction that developed exceptions to the crime of abortion via the common law, most notably the case of *R v Davidson*. Similarly, in New South Wales the District Court followed (and expanded upon) the Menhennitt ruling in the 1971 case of *R v Wald*, which provided for an exception to the crime of abortion where continuation of the pregnancy posed a danger to the pregnant person's health. An example of legislative exceptions to the crime of abortion may also be found in the law of South Australia where, prior to abortion law reform in 2021, legislation set out these exceptions in circumstances where a pregnant person's health or life was endangered or where there was evidence of a serious issue of foetal abnormality.

Accordingly, even when abortion was a crime, it was still legally available due to the exceptions that developed to enable legal access. Nevertheless, the paradigm shift that has transferred abortion across Australia from the criminal law to a matter of health regulation is significant for a number of reasons. These include the advancement of conceptualisations of abortion as a human right in the domestic sphere, the eradication of legal ambiguity, and challenging the stigma that remains attached to abortion.

Why Is Decriminalisation Important?

One of the reasons why the decriminalisation of abortion is important is because abortion cannot be a right if it is a crime. We have already examined the increasing focus of the international human rights regime on access to abortion as an issue that is fundamental to the human rights of a pregnant person, but it is worth reiterating that the significance of recognising abortion as a human right goes hand in hand with accepting that it cannot be a crime under Australian law.

The eradication of legal ambiguity is another reason why decriminalisation is important. When abortion is a crime and simultaneously is widely available, as was the case in much of Australia prior to the decriminalisation of abortion nationwide, there is ambiguity and uncertainty around its legal status. This is problematic for a few reasons, as I have discussed in other writings on this topic.[10] First, this lack of clarity results in a depiction of the law as foolish, and inconsistency in enforcement weakens respect for the rule of law. Even a preschool child knows this. If I tell my five-year-old that, pursuant to the rules of the house, she is not allowed to draw on the walls, and if she does so the resulting penalty will be iPad confiscation, but each time she draws on the walls the penalty is not enforced, she will surely lose respect for the house rules. Therefore, notwithstanding the reality that prosecutions did occur, the fact that so few prosecutions took place relative to the actual provision of abortion services diminished law's status within the community.

A second concern relating to the rule of law is that people should be able to understand what the law is so they know if they are violating it. If abortion is a crime but is still widely legally available, this creates confusion for both medical practitioners and pregnant people regarding the legality of abortion. In fact, it was the 1998 arrest of two doctors for performing an unlawful abortion that triggered the initial liberalisation of Western Australia's abortion laws (before abortion was fully decriminalised in that state in September 2023). The doctors were charged with performing an abortion on a woman in Perth in November 1996, after her child revealed to a school class that the home refrigerator contained foetal remains—the woman was planning to take the remains back to New Zealand to be buried according to a custom of her family. Despite the fact that the charges were ultimately dropped, the prosecution of these doctors created a climate of fear among the state's medical profession such that 'medical termination procedures were suspended and women were forced either to continue unwanted pregnancies, fly interstate to access medical procedures, or perform abortions upon themselves'.[11] Against this background Western Australia liberalised its abortion laws in a first step towards decriminalising abortion, stopping short of a complete removal of abortion from the criminal law.

While this case illustrates that criminalising abortion may lead to fear and uncertainty among doctors regarding the circumstances in which an abortion may lawfully be performed, such confusion may also exist among ordinary Australians. This is illustrated in the 2010 Queensland case of *R v Brennan and Leach*. Tegan Leach, aged twenty-one, and Sergei Brennan, twenty-two, asked Brennan's sister in Ukraine to post them the drugs required to carry out a medical abortion. Medically induced abortion, also known as 'medical abortion' or 'medication abortion', refers to a non-surgical abortion. In Australia, it is only available to terminate pregnancies up to nine weeks' gestation and is carried out using a combination of the drugs mifepristone and misoprostol. The medication required for a medical abortion was only included by the Therapeutic Goods Administration (TGA) on the Register of Therapeutic Goods in 2012. Therefore, in 2010, when this case was heard, it was difficult to access medical abortion in Australia. Police discovered the drugs during a house search (for unrelated reasons) and Brennan and Leach were prosecuted under the sections of the Queensland *Criminal Code* that enshrined the crime of abortion.

Brennan and Leach's ignorance of the law is clear from the openness of their behaviour. They did not attempt to import the drugs covertly but did so overtly, via the regular postal system with a Customs declaration. When interviewed by police, they did not request legal representation and were open about their motivation to import the drugs in order to terminate Leach's pregnancy—they were unaware they were confessing to a crime. Such was the confusing state of affairs created by the availability of abortion that coexisted with its status as a crime. The outcome of the case did little to clarify the law, as Leach was acquitted on the basis that the drugs ingested were noxious to the foetus and not to her, and therefore did not technically violate the relevant provision, which stated that: 'Any woman who, with intent to procure her own miscarriage … unlawfully administers to herself any poison or other noxious thing … is guilty of a crime.' Brennan was also acquitted on the basis that it would create a legal anomaly if he was convicted when Leach had been acquitted. Accordingly, the case served to further highlight the uncertainty and confusion surrounding the legality of abortion in circumstances where abortion is a crime but is nevertheless available and broadly accepted by the community as an important form of health care.

Much has been written about the fact that the law can promote the stigmatisation of certain behaviours or characteristics but, conversely, can also aid the removal of stigmatisation.[12] So another reason why the decriminalisation of abortion is important is because its criminalisation exacerbates its taboo status. If one accepts that labelling abortion as a crime enhances its stigma, and that people accessing abortion services should not be stigmatised, then it seems clear that the appropriate medium for regulating abortion services is via legislation that regulates health care, not legislation that criminalises (and demonises) those seeking access to health care. As abortion law expert Rebecca Cook asserts, when a state criminalises abortion, 'it is constructing its social meaning as inherently wrong and harmful to society ... In contrast, the legal framing of abortion as a health issue constructs meanings of preservation and promotion of health.'[13]

Nevertheless, while the decriminalisation of abortion may be a precondition of its de-stigmatisation, the shift from a criminal law approach to a health law approach does not guarantee the complete eradication of stigma. The stigma of abortion stems from more than law. It is embedded in social attitudes towards religion, pregnancy and gender. Changes to law alone are not sufficient to dismantle deeply ingrained attitudes and perspectives. So abortion stigma may prevail even when abortion itself has been decriminalised. Recently in Australia there has even been a trend towards 'normalising and celebratory depictions of abortion'.[14] However, regrettably, this has failed to lead to an eradication of abortion stigma in Australia, even when coupled with decriminalisation. So while decriminalisation of abortion is an important step, one should be careful not to overstate what it can achieve.

Fortunately, in Australia, the decriminalisation of abortion has been a first rather than final step. Other legal mechanisms have been put in place to help facilitate access to abortion, including measures to mitigate the impact of conscientious objection and the introduction of safe access zones around abortion clinics.

Matters of Conscience

The decriminalisation of abortion removes the primary legal barrier to abortion access, but traditionally, health professionals with a conscientious objection to abortion have been legally permitted to refrain from participating in the provision of abortion services. There is no doubt that some people hold sincere, genuine beliefs in the immorality of abortion. These should be respected and consideration given to avoiding the infliction of moral distress on such individuals by compelling them to act against their conscience. At the same time, a legally enshrined right to conscientious objection is another way in which the law acts as an impediment to abortion access. Allowing health professionals to completely abstain from participating creates a situation where pregnant people may have no-one to turn to when seeking access to the full range of reproductive health services. Accordingly, the WHO has expressed the view that conscientious objection 'continues to operate as a barrier to access to quality abortion care ... If it proves impossible to regulate conscientious objection in a way that respects, protects and fulfils abortion seekers' rights, conscientious objection in abortion provision may become indefensible.'[15]

To facilitate an appropriate balance between the right to conscientious objection and the right to terminate a pregnancy, all Australian jurisdictions require a health professional to provide the service in an emergency. Further, all jurisdictions except the Australian Capital Territory have imposed what is known as an 'obligation to refer' on a health professional with a conscientious objection to abortion. The obligation to refer does not require a literal medical referral; rather, it requires a health professional with a conscientious objection to direct a patient seeking information about abortion to someone without a conscientious objection. For example, in Victoria, a doctor with a conscientious objection could direct a patient to Family Planning Victoria, MSI Australia (formerly known as Marie Stopes Australia), the Fertility Control Clinic, or another doctor who does not conscientiously object to abortion.

Other countries take a much stronger approach to safeguarding access to abortion services. Some take the view that conscientious objection should not be permitted at all—that a person with a conscientious objection to abortion should not specialise in a field of medicine where abortion is integral to the provision of patient care. This position is reflected in the laws of Sweden, for example. In comparison to such an approach, the imposition of an obligation to refer seems like a fairly minimalist obligation aimed at ensuring continuity of health care and preventing patients from being left in the lurch, with no-one to turn to in their time of need. This is especially important for vulnerable or marginalised patients whose access to health care may already be compromised, such as patients with limited English-language proficiency, minors, or those living in remote areas.

Nevertheless, when the legislation to reform Victoria's abortion law was being debated, the obligation to refer was the subject of significant controversy, with the archbishop of Melbourne threatening to close the maternity departments in Catholic hospitals if these provisions were enacted. The expressed concern was that a referral renders a person with a conscientious objection complicit in the act, thereby forcing them to act against their conscience. This threat was not carried out, but there is general acceptance of the right of institutions, such as Catholic hospitals, to refuse to provide abortion services. Accordingly, conscientious objection is invoked by institutions as well as individual health professionals. This is contentious, as many people dispute the view that an institution can have a conscience, positing that such a right can only belong to an individual. It is also contentious because it allows faith-based hospitals that are also public hospitals, funded by the public purse, to refuse to provide abortion services.

The following story, recently reported in *The Guardian*, illustrates this point:

In Brisbane, in January 2021, Amy was devastated when a genetic screening test during her first trimester showed a high likelihood of Edwards syndrome. Babies born with this chromosomal condition typically do not survive longer than a week after birth. A scan at the Mater hospital, where she was receiving maternity care, confirmed the sad news. 'They were really emphasising that the condition is incompatible with life and leading to the conclusion that termination was the best option, without saying it themselves,' Amy recalls …

Amy was told that Mater hospital would not perform her termination due to its Catholic affiliation. She had received excellent care from the Mater during her first pregnancy, with a difficult delivery. 'To have been cared for by them in that situation and turfed out by them in this scenario … when the dust had settled, I was furious that religion was calling the shots.'

Amy did not want to put herself through the stress of waiting weeks for a termination in the public system. She had the procedure days later at a private clinic, at an out-of-pocket cost of hundreds of dollars, and struggled to process the loss of a wanted baby.[16]

Legislation throughout Australia is silent on the subject of institutional conscientious objection, yet there is tacit acceptance of this in practice. Fiona Patten, leader of the Reason Party and a member of the Victorian Legislative Council between 2014 and 2022, introduced a Bill into the Victorian Parliament in 2022 to try and change this. Unfortunately, the Bill did not get the support of the major parties. Patten's Bill, if it had been passed, would have imposed an obligation on all public hospitals, including those that are faith-based, to provide health services relating to contraception, abortion and voluntary assisted dying.

Back in 2019, when Tanya Plibersek was the federal shadow minister for women, she indicated that the Australian Labor Party would tie funding to public hospitals to a willingness to provide abortion services. However, that policy was dumped by the Albanese Labor government. A consequence of the ability of institutions, including faith-based public hospitals, to conscientiously object to abortions is that in some states, such as Victoria, most abortions are provided through the private sector, once again exposing those who are most vulnerable. This is unacceptable—indeed, it would not be accepted for any other form of health care.

The Australian Capital Territory has recently acted on this issue. An inquiry into abortion services conducted in April 2023 was critical of the Catholic-run Calvary Public Hospital's refusal to provide abortion services. In response, the government compulsorily acquired the hospital to ensure the provision of the full range of reproductive health services. It remains to be seen whether other jurisdictions will pressure denominational public hospitals to provide abortion services in the absence of federal pressure to do so.

Safe Access Zones

In 2013, Tasmania passed legislation to decriminalise abortion in that state, including a provision that provided for safe access zones of 150 metres around places providing abortion services. As the name suggests, safe access zones provide a zone through which people can safely enter a clinic providing abortion services, free of intimidation or harassment. Most Australian legislation uses this term, but the zones are also sometimes referred to as 'bubble zones' because they create a safety bubble around an abortion clinic; 'buffer zones' because they create a buffer between patients and anti-abortion picketers; or 'exclusion zones' because they exclude anti-abortion conduct from occurring within a specified zone.

Section 9 of the Tasmanian legislation prevents people from engaging in 'prohibited behaviour' within 150 metres of a clinic at which terminations are provided, with a penalty of a fine of up to and including 75 penalty units and/or imprisonment for a term not exceeding twelve months. Prohibited behaviour includes harassment, intimidation or obstruction of a person; visible anti-abortion conduct; footpath interference; and recording a person entering the premises.

Following Tasmania's lead, the other Australian jurisdictions saw the merit in safe access zone provisions and enacted their own. Some, like Victoria and the Australian Capital Territory, had already decriminalised abortion, and in 2015 both of these jurisdictions passed subsequent legislation to enshrine safe access zones. Others, like New South Wales, South Australia and Western Australia, provided for safe access zones before fully decriminalising abortion. A third category, specifically the Northern Territory and Queensland, included safe access zone provisions as part of their legislation decriminalising abortion.

Safe access zones protect patients, staff and support persons from encountering anti-abortion conduct when seeking to access clinics that provide abortion services. Such conduct may range from being quite passive to very active conduct. Silent prayers and vigils are an example of passive conduct, which nevertheless communicates judgement and disapproval, causing harm to patients. Active obstructive conduct includes barricading the doors of a clinic to physically prevent access. Other forms of anti-abortion conduct that sit along the spectrum include holding up posters depicting images of foetuses at various stages of gestation, and attempts to verbally dissuade patients from accessing abortion by calling them murderers.

Before the introduction of safe access zones, many Australian clinics, especially standalone identifiable centres that did not form part of a more general hospital, were confronted with the regular presence of anti-abortion activists on their doorsteps, whose conduct included the following:

(a) Protesters approaching, following or walking alongside people approaching clinic premises, distributing pamphlets, and distributing plastic models of foetuses.

(b) Protesters equating foetuses with babies by imploring patients not to 'kill' their 'baby', and castigating patients as murderers ...

(e) Protesters displaying large and graphic posters depicting what [they] purported to be foetuses post-abortion, foetuses in buckets, or skulls of foetuses.

(f) Protesters distributing visually graphic literature containing medically inaccurate and misleading information warning that abortion results in infertility, failed relationships, mental illness and cancer.[17]

This created an extremely unpleasant working environment for staff at the clinics, which frequently took its toll on staff health and wellbeing. For patients, the impact of such conduct ranged from stress and distress in the moment, to delaying or even deterring them from accessing a lawful medical service, which of course was the objective of the conduct. The medical director of MSI Australia remarked in an interview that 'we had patients coming in in tears, distraught, upset, just because of the way they were treated and were made to feel by the protesters'.[18]

Thankfully, empirical research I have conducted (with Associate Professor Tania Penovic) suggests that in Australia, safe access zones are achieving their objective of protecting patient health, safety, wellbeing, privacy and dignity. The zones are keeping anti-abortion conduct away from the clinics and are sending a strong message of support for patient autonomy, equality, and their right to access the full range of reproductive health services free of stigma and shame. This is in line with the human rights approach discussed earlier in this book.

Unfortunately, the journey has not all been smooth sailing, with a constitutional challenge to the Tasmanian and Victorian safe access zone provisions taking place in the case of *Clubb v Edwards; Preston v*

Avery (2019) 366 ALR 1. In April 2015, John Preston was found guilty of engaging in prohibited behaviour within a Tasmanian safe access zone. He was fined $3000 for picketing outside a Hobart clinic. In Victoria in 2016, Kathleen Clubb became the first person to be convicted under that state's safe access zone provisions after she approached two people walking into the East Melbourne Fertility Control Clinic and attempted to hand them anti-abortion pamphlets. She was charged with engaging in prohibited behaviour within a Victorian safe access zone and was fined $5000.

Clubb and Preston challenged the Victorian and Tasmanian provisions, arguing they violated the freedom of political communication implied in the federal Constitution. In the absence of a constitutional Bill of rights, this is the closest thing we have to a constitutionally enshrined right to free speech, but it is much narrower in its scope. Fortunately, the High Court of Australia affirmed the constitutional validity of both the Tasmanian and Victorian safe access zone provisions, thereby ensuring that people in need of abortion services can continue to access the full range of reproductive healthcare services in Victoria and Tasmania (and by comity, other jurisdictions) free of intimidation and harassment. This decision was a victory for reproductive rights, with the court explicitly noting the legitimacy of laws whose objective is to protect the safety, wellbeing, privacy and dignity of people accessing a lawful medical service.

BARRIERS TO ACCESS

While Australia has made huge strides in the advancement of reproductive rights, the march towards the realisation of full reproductive justice continues, with several barriers to abortion access still to be dismantled. These include the sometimes problematic attitudes of health professionals coupled with deficiencies in medical training; a continued focus on gestational limits in most Australian jurisdictions; and financial and geographic obstacles.

Gestational Limits

One of the key remaining legal barriers to abortion access in Australia relates to gestational limits. Abortion 'on request' is available in all Australian jurisdictions. This means that across the country, a pregnant person can request an abortion without providing the reason why they would like to terminate the pregnancy. However, only the Australian Capital Territory allows abortion on request at any stage of gestation—subject to the professional willingness and ability of the medical practitioners involved. In all other jurisdictions there is a gestational limit to abortion on request. For example, in Victoria, the gestational limit for abortion on request is twenty-four weeks' gestation, but a person who is more than twenty-four weeks' pregnant may nevertheless terminate a pregnancy if two medical practitioners believe that abortion is appropriate in the medical, physical, psychological and social circumstances. In Tasmania, however, the gestational limit for abortion on request is much earlier, at sixteen weeks.

One may wonder why it matters. If abortion is still available at a later gestation, and available for a wide range of circumstances at that, why does it matter if it is not available 'on request'? Adding to that the fact that in Australia the vast majority of abortions occur in the first trimester, why focus on an aspect of the law that only affects a limited number of people? The discussion below draws on previous research of mine that considers this question.[19]

First, there is the issue of so-called reproductive tourism, which I mentioned earlier in this book. We have seen this in the surrogacy context, where many Australians travel overseas each year to access compensated surrogacy arrangements that are illegal back home. Reproductive tourism, or forum shopping, is an inevitable corollary of laws that restrict access. This in turn exacerbates socio-economic and geographic disparities in access as people who either live in a more liberal jurisdiction or who are able to travel to that jurisdiction can access abortion services that remain inaccessible to others. So, whereas the situation in Australia is not comparable to that of the United States, where numerous states have banned abortion and reproductive tourism abounds, it is nevertheless worth mentioning.

The second reason why gestational limits to abortion on request matter is because they undermine the health law approach to abortion by encouraging rushed decision-making. They also use arbitrary measures to regulate abortion differently to other medical procedures, where informed consent and professional willingness and ability are the only legal criteria. Such an approach also serves to enhance socio-economic disparities in access, as people who are in a position to obtain expeditious private medical care are less affected by gestational limits than those who are disadvantaged by geographic or socio-economic status. Further, treating abortion differently to other medical procedures is inherently discriminatory against people who may become pregnant and has the effect of exacerbating the stigma attached to abortion.

Third, gestational limits place the burden on the pregnant person to justify their decision to terminate the pregnancy, and what's more, they give the medical practitioner the power to evaluate that justification and determine whether it is acceptable to have an abortion. This exacerbates the existing power dynamic between the doctor and the patient. Further, there is a distinctly gendered dimension to this power differential. Gestational limits infantilise women, reinforce stereotypes of women as weak and vulnerable, call into question their capacity to make important and rational decisions, and compromise their right to bodily autonomy and integrity.

Deborah's recollection of her abortion in the early 1970s in Victoria, when it was still a criminal offence but subject to a health exception, illustrates this point. She recalls that she

> needed the mandatory psychiatric report and recommendation, and this was perhaps the most revolting aspect of the experience. I was sexually molested by the psychiatrist, and had to pay him cash on the spot. He knew my future depended on his report, that, in a sense, my life was in his hands. If I was forced to continue with the pregnancy my parents would disown me and I'd be sacked by the

Education Department as unmarried mothers were against all regulations at that time. I was not in a position to resist the psychiatrist's advances, and also too young to understand fully what the role of a psychiatrist involved.[20]

This is an extreme example of the power that law and medicine combined exercise over patients when abortion is only allowed where, in the opinion of the doctor, there is a risk to the health of the pregnant person. Thankfully, much has changed since this time. Nationwide abortion is no longer a crime but is available 'on request' in all jurisdictions. But the fact that, other than in the Australian Capital Territory, the availability of abortion on request is capped at a certain stage of gestation, increases the risk of this sort of conduct. The scales of power are already tipped heavily in favour of the doctor, who can choose to refuse to participate in an abortion. Giving doctors the legal power to evaluate a patient's reason for wishing to terminate the pregnancy in my view increases this power differential to an unacceptable extent. Deborah's story clearly illustrates the power imbalance between a patient and doctor when a doctor is given the authority to determine whether termination of pregnancy is justified in the circumstances.

If abortion is conceptualised as health care—as it should be, and as the paradigm shift from a criminal law approach to a health law approach suggests is the intention of Australian lawmakers—then it is illogical to retain an approach to abortion that requires the patient to justify their decision at a certain stage of gestation. Further, the requirement for *two* medical practitioners to agree on the appropriateness of the abortion once the gestational limit for abortion on request has been reached—as is the case in all jurisdictions with legislatively enshrined gestational limits—significantly exacerbates the power dynamic and may cause considerable stress and distress. This is particularly the case in rural and remote areas where there may be added challenges to finding two doctors. Therefore, in my view, Australian jurisdictions should follow the lead of the Australian Capital Territory and remove gestational limits for abortion on request. At the very least, the requirement for two medical practitioners to authorise the procedure should be dropped.

Medical Training and the Attitudes of Health Professionals

Access to abortion services requires a reasonable cohort of medical practitioners who are willing and able to provide the service. The willingness of doctors to provide abortion services is discussed below, but one should not make assumptions with respect to capability. As I have considered elsewhere, abortion has been neglected in medical curricula and doctor training.[21] This vacuum is to some extent attributable to the fact that abortion has historically been a crime. And while improvements to medical education and training have been made over the years, a deficit remains. As such, a 2020 study of final-year medical students across Australia concluded that

> while abortion care is taught in most Australian medical schools, structured and standardised teaching is still lacking. Students' confidence around abortion care is inadequate, and the majority of students showed a strong desire to have more direct abortion placement exposure. The current Australian medical curriculum will need to expand in significant ways in order to equip new graduates with [the] necessary skills to provide basic and safe care for women requesting induced abortion.[22]

This is not a uniquely Australian problem, with deficits in training and education existing in many other developed countries, including the United States, Canada, United Kingdom and Norway. But it is a problem that must be rectified if we are serious about providing high-quality abortion care nationwide.

In the context of abortions after eighteen weeks' gestation, which require a higher skill level to perform, inadequate practitioner training and expertise combined with other factors, such as a lack of practitioner willingness to provide these later gestation abortions, have resulted in a significant nationwide shortage of providers. Patients in need of later abortions are typically the most vulnerable; they may be carrying foetuses with severe abnormalities only detected at the twenty-week scan; they may be victims of domestic violence who are unable to access health care at the time of their choosing; they may be people with intellectual disabilities who are unaware of their pregnancy until it becomes obvious to all. These are the people most in need of support, and they are the people most likely to be denied such support due to a lack of adequately trained health professionals who are willing and able to provide the service they require.

The impact of this skill deficit is compounded by negative practitioner attitudes. As already discussed, the law throughout Australia allows a health professional with a conscientious objection to abortion to refuse to participate. The rates of conscientious objection to abortion in Australia are not as high as in some other countries. Further, research indicates that these rates are lower in Australia than for voluntary assisted dying, which since 2017 has been legal in every Australian state. Nevertheless, a significant minority of Australian health professionals conscientiously object to abortion, with a 2018 online survey of the fellows and specialist trainees of the Royal Australian and New Zealand College of Obstetricians and Gynaecologists finding that of the 632 respondents, almost 14 per cent opposed abortion for reasons of conscience.[23] This is enough to have an impact, especially in rural or remote areas where the only doctor in reasonable geographic proximity to a pregnant person may be a doctor with a conscientious objection.

While even relatively low rates of conscientious objection may have an impact on the ability of a pregnant person to access abortion services, this is compounded when health professionals refuse to comply with the legal obligation to refer a patient to someone without such an objection. On this point, researchers in 2019 found that a 'significant minority (15%) of practitioners who claim a CO [conscientious objection] do not adhere to obligations to refer, but instead attempt to delay or deny access'.[24] This is not only true of individual medical practitioners but also of pharmacists and institutions. It may take the form, for example, of doctors ordering unnecessary tests or scans to delay access, suggestions that patients take some time to consider their decision in circumstances where time is of the essence, or a more direct refusal to refer a patient to another health professional.

Recognising there are clearly health professionals with a sincere and genuine conscientious objection to abortion, the aforementioned researchers also found there are health professionals who falsely claim conscientious objection simply to avoid abortion service provision. They may refuse to participate in an abortion because they want to avoid the stigma of being labelled an abortion provider, particularly in areas with high rates of conscientious objection. This is yet another reason why it is imperative to dismantle the stigma associated with abortion.

Further, harmful conduct experienced by health professionals may go beyond stigma. It is difficult to blame a doctor who fears becoming an abortion provider because they do not want to be the target of hate mail, or they do not want their children to be bullied at school. The introduction of safe access zones has gone a long way towards protecting health professionals working at abortion clinics from being targeted and subjected to anti-abortion picketing, but anti-abortion activists may have a negative impact in other ways. This is especially so in contexts where small-town gossip can quickly lead to social ostracism.

Accordingly, the law can take us some way in combatting the impact of negative attitudes towards abortion, such as imposing an obligation to refer on conscientious objectors and establishing safe access zones around abortion clinics. However, until abortion becomes destigmatised, there will be health professionals who remain unwilling to participate even in the absence of a conscientious objection.

Geographic Barriers

In May 2023, the Senate Community Affairs References Committee handed down a report titled *Ending the Postcode Lottery: Addressing Barriers to Sexual, Maternity and Reproductive Healthcare in Australia*. This report was the result of a Senate inquiry into barriers to achieving universal access to sexual and reproductive health information, treatment and services. The title is instructive because it foregrounds what has become known as the 'postcode lottery' in access to reproductive health care. In Australia today, a person's access to the full range of reproductive health services to a large extent depends on where they live. This is the case not only with respect to abortion but also, for example, contraception and maternity care. Discrepancies in access based on geography depend not only on the fact that different jurisdictions have differing legal frameworks. Evidence was presented to the inquiry confirming what those working in this field have been proclaiming for years: that people living in rural and remote areas may face significant challenges when trying to access abortion services— especially regarding surgical terminations, the only option available after nine weeks' gestation.

The consequences of inadequate services include people having to travel significant distances to access the health care they require, or forfeiting that health care altogether if such travel is not a realistic option. The disadvantages faced by people in rural and remote areas are compounded when those people are also affected by other vulnerabilities. For example, people from culturally and linguistically diverse backgrounds, people with disabilities or people experiencing family violence may confront additional complexities when trying to access abortion services.

The absence of a requirement that public hospitals provide the full range of reproductive health services is problematic, as there are large parts of Australia where there is no private provision of services. This is an issue that is relevant in several contexts. Earlier, I discussed my concerns about allowing faith-based public hospitals to engage in institutional conscientious objection. The Senate committee's report stopped short of recommending that public hospitals be required to provide abortion services, recommending instead that 'all public hospitals within Australia be equipped to provide surgical pregnancy terminations, or timely and affordable pathways to other local providers'. A Senate inquiry is, by its very nature, a political process, so a report stemming from such an inquiry is the result of negotiation and compromise. It strikes me as likely that this recommendation represents such a compromise. If adopted, it would be an improvement on the current situation, but in a country that prides itself on universal public health care, public hospitals should provide the full range of reproductive health care, not just be equipped to provide such care or facilitate it in other health facilities.

An article in *The Age* newspaper published in August 2023 reported on the lack of abortion services in rural and remote Victoria.[25] According to this article, there are seventeen local government areas with no abortion access—known as 'abortion deserts'—and this is a troubling statistic. People living in these areas have to travel, sometimes for hours to access the necessary services. In other parts of Australia, such as northern Queensland and northern New South Wales, access is also extremely challenging or non-existent. We know this problem exists; in fact, we have known this for some time. It needs to be properly addressed.

Aspects of this issue are complex and debatable. Should the right to conscientious objection be removed in circumstances where the doctor with such an objection is the only doctor in town? And if this approach was adopted, would this only serve to exacerbate the existing medical skill shortage in rural areas, because objectors might move to urban areas to avoid having to act against their conscience? Would it result in pregnant people being treated poorly by conscientious objectors who were being compelled to provide the service? In my view, a first and obvious step is to require public hospitals to provide abortion services. Individual medical practitioners would still be allowed to refuse to participate based on conscientious objection, but not whole institutions, which are funded by the taxpayer and whose refusal to provide this service means that entire regions are left lacking essential healthcare services.

Financial Barriers

States are responsible for the provision of abortion services in Australia's public hospitals, while federal funding is available via Medicare and the Pharmaceutical Benefits Scheme (PBS) to subsidise the cost of abortions performed in the private sector. Inadequate public provision of abortion services in most of Australia (with the notable exception of Adelaide, where services are available from the Pregnancy Advisory Centre as well as most public hospitals), and the high costs—combined with unsatisfactory subsidisation—of abortions performed in the private realm, have created significant financial barriers to access.

As noted in the *Ending the Postcode Lottery* report, the lack of adequate public funding for abortion, combined with the refusal of several public hospitals to provide abortion services, has resulted in most abortions being provided within the private system. This has led to notable cost discrepancies between providers and jurisdictions, and a situation in which abortion is financially out of reach for many people. A medical abortion may cost less than $20 where providers bulk-bill and the patient has a healthcare card, or it may cost hundreds of dollars, despite the fact that the drugs required are included on the PBS and could be limited to an out-of-pocket cost of approximately $30.

For example, MSI Australia, a national provider with a network of nine clinics, charges a minimum of:

- $325 for people with a Medicare card obtaining a medical abortion by telehealth
- $620 for people with a Medicare card obtaining a medical abortion in a clinic
- $730 for people with a Medicare card obtaining a surgical abortion (all abortions after nine weeks' gestation).

These costs are in addition to indirect costs such as travel expenses, childcare arrangements and time off work. My intention here is not to single out or criticise one provider of abortion services. Rather, it is to emphasise that it is not acceptable that people seeking to terminate a pregnancy are confronted with these sorts of costs to access the health care that they require—certainly not in a county that represents itself as providing universal access to publicly funded health care.

With respect to surgical abortions, the price increases with the stage of gestation at which the abortion is performed, to account for the increased complexities involved in performing a later termination and the lack of medical practitioners willing and able to do so. Terminations carried out at later gestations can cost in excess of $7000. A centre manager at a clinic providing abortion services described the way in which the cost increases as follows: 'Well, the cost goes up in increments every week, which is part of our structure and the way that the payments are. But it goes up to, like, with [a] Medicare Card, up to seven and a half thousand dollars at 24 weeks, which is a huge amount of money.'[26] This was in 2017, so the cost may have increased since then. Considering that people requiring later terminations are frequently the most vulnerable members of our society, and those least able to afford the cost, this is a particularly cruel irony.

Some other countries seem to do things better: in England and Portugal, abortions are provided at no cost by the respective national health services. Domestically, the Australian Capital Territory recently took matters into its own hands. In April 2023, it made abortion up to sixteen weeks' gestation free to all residents of that jurisdiction. It is now time for the rest of the country to follow suit.

While I have spoken about geographic barriers to abortion access as separate from financial barriers, the two are in fact linked. People living in rural or remote areas, or those who live in jurisdictions with a more restrictive legal framework, may need to travel to access abortion services, and this frequently results in additional transportation and accommodation costs. Further, financial and geographic disadvantage often compound other vulnerabilities, leading to presentations at a clinic at a later stage of gestation, and an additional financial burden and potential complications that are a corollary of later gestation abortions. These barriers are further linked with problematic practitioner attitudes and training—if a pregnant person lives in a rural or remote area where the only doctor in town has a conscientious objection to abortion, this may result in delayed access to care and a corresponding increase in the cost of the abortion.

RECENT DEVELOPMENTS

There have been both positive and negative recent developments in the federal and state domains. Three worth focusing on are improvements in access to medical abortion, attempts to pass anti-abortion legislation, and reforms to Western Australia's abortion law.

Medical Abortion

In Australia, medical abortion via the drugs mifepristone and misoprostol is available up to nine weeks' gestation, but some new developments are flowing from the *Ending the Postcode Lottery* report. Pursuant to Recommendation 20, access to medical abortion would be improved by expanding the range of practitioners allowed to facilitate a medical termination of pregnancy and reducing the training requirements for prescribing practitioners and dispensing pharmacists. These requirements are applied to abortion medication but not other medications requiring specialised knowledge, such as diabetes medication, thereby contributing to abortion's 'exceptional' status.

By way of background, medical abortion in Australia has a complicated and politicised history, despite being included on the WHO's list of essential medicines. In 1996, political negotiations between the government of the day and senator Brian Harradine, known for his anti-abortion views, led the federal parliament to pass legislation referred to as the 'Harradine Amendment'. This ensured that mifepristone could only be imported into Australia with the written permission of the federal minister for health, creating a significant obstacle to the availability of medical abortion in Australia.

In 2006, federal parliament finally repealed the Harradine Amendment, removing the ministerial veto power over the importation of the necessary medication. This was a notable step forward. But mifepristone was still not included on the Australian Register of Therapeutic Goods and was therefore only available through the TGA's Authorised Prescriber Scheme. This was a cumbersome process and only a handful of doctors, generally (and predictably) located in urban areas, received authorisation to import and prescribe the medication.

In August 2012, the TGA finally agreed to include mifepristone on the register. This enabled medical practitioners in general to prescribe the drugs required for a medical abortion, as opposed to only those who had been authorised pursuant to the Authorised Prescriber process. And in June 2013, mifepristone was included on the PBS, thereby (at least in theory) securing its affordability. Nevertheless, the drugs required for a medical abortion were still treated differently to other drugs, as doctors and pharmacists were required to undertake specific training and a special registration process in order to prescribe and dispense them. The consequence of this burden was, predictably, that few doctors and pharmacists engaged with the process, and there has therefore been a lack of medical professionals able to facilitate a medical termination of pregnancy.

In July 2023, following the recommendations of the Senate inquiry, the TGA announced significant changes aimed at increasing access to medical abortion in Australia. It removed the extra training and certification/registration requirements that had been imposed on prescribers and pharmacists dispensing the necessary medication. The exceptional status that had been imposed on the drugs required for a medical abortion up to this point was removed, with this medication now subject to the same rules and processes as other medications. It is hoped that, with the added burden on GPs and pharmacies now removed, a greater number of GPs will be willing to prescribe, and more pharmacies willing to dispense, the medication.

In addition, the changes also allow nurse practitioners to prescribe the drugs for a medical abortion, enhancing the number of people able to facilitate a termination of pregnancy. This is a particularly significant change for people living in rural and remote areas, where access to GP or specialist care may be limited.[27] These changes combined will hopefully have a notable impact on improving access to abortion in Australia. This is what occurred in Canada, which deregulated access to medical abortion back in 2017. The number of abortion providers in Canada is increasing significantly, which is in step with global trends suggesting that the proportion of people opting for medical (as opposed to surgical) abortion is also steadily increasing.

Finally, I should note that the increased use of tele-health during the COVID-19 pandemic also served to enhance the accessibility of medical abortion. During the pandemic, the federal government made some adjustments to the Medicare Benefits Schedule to encourage the use of telehealth, in an effort to restrict transmission of COVID-19. As result, medical abortion via telehealth became a more affordable option for many Australians. Further, it made abortion services much more attainable for people living in rural or remote areas, or those who faced challenges leaving home. These new Medicare item numbers were due to expire at the time of writing, and it was unclear whether they would be extended, but I hope they are. Medical abortion facilitated via telehealth and subsidised by Medicare creates an alternative pathway for abortion for those who are in particularly vulnerable situations and cannot easily access a clinic. While telehealth may have its problems and may not be a panacea (for example, it is harder to establish a relationship of trust via telehealth, and it may be harder for health professionals to detect issues such as domestic violence via telehealth), it is important that we retain this option for those who most need it.

Attempts to Erode Reproductive Rights

On 30 November 2022, the Human Rights (Children Born Alive Protection) Bill was introduced into the Senate by senators Matthew Canavan, Alex Antic and Ralph Babet. The focus of this Bill is later gestation abortions. For context, it should be noted that according to the Royal Australian and New Zealand College of Obstetricians and Gynaecologists, abortion after twenty weeks' gestation—the subject of the Bill—constitutes approximately 1 per cent of all abortions, so the Bill is directed at an uncommon scenario. Pursuant to the Bill's explanatory memorandum, the 'purpose of this bill is to enhance Australia's human rights protections for children by ensuring that all children are afforded the same medical care and treatment as any other person, including those born alive as a result of a termination'. The Bill purports to address the very rare situation in which a later-gestation abortion procedure results in an infant showing signs of life outside the uterus. In the vast majority of cases, standard evidence-based medical practice dictates that feticide is part of the process for performing a later-gestation abortion. Therefore, of those 1 per cent of abortions that occur after twenty weeks' gestation, standard medical practice is to ensure there is no prospect of an infant being born alive.

In certain rare circumstances, a decision is made not to include feticide as part of the abortion procedure, and this may result in an infant showing signs of life. This tends to occur in the most tragic of cases; for example, in situations involving a wanted pregnancy, where tests indicate that the foetus has a condition incompatible with life but the pregnant person wants the opportunity to hold and comfort the baby in its final hours. In such a situation, clinical practice dictates that health professionals provide palliative care to the baby and ensure that all efforts are made to avoid pain and suffering. Legislation prescribing this practice is unnecessary, and falsely implies that without such legislation, the provision of care is inadequate. Further, a requirement to provide life-sustaining treatment in these circumstances, where death is inevitable, contravenes best medical practice. Therefore, the Bill is at best unnecessary and at worst attempts to compel medical practitioners to engage in conduct that contravenes best practice.

I was ambivalent about mentioning this Bill in this book. In part, I wanted to exclude it on the basis that the Bill represents a coopting of both US-style anti-choice advocacy and human rights language that fundamentally misrepresents the reality of clinical practice and the approach of human rights law. Further, the Bill is doomed to fail, or at least is highly unlikely to get the votes needed to pass, so why bother discussing it? But another part of me felt that in order to provide a full picture of the state of reproductive rights in Australia, it is important to include circumstances in which reproductive rights have been eroded, or where there are ongoing attempts to do so. This Bill is little more than a thinly veiled attempt to erode reproductive rights in Australia by further stigmatising later-gestation abortions and regulating areas of clinical practice that do not require regulation.

In February 2023, the Senate referred the Bill to the Community Affairs Legislation Committee for inquiry, which heard evidence from several experts testifying to its problematic nature. The committee released its report in August 2023, expressing concern with the constitutional and human rights issues posed by the Bill. The committee also noted the existing regulatory framework and the undesirability of placing 'additional obligations on already highly regulated healthcare professionals, without providing any benefit to patient safety or quality of care'. To the contrary, the committee recognised that the availability of abortion and pregnancy support services could be negatively affected were such additional legal obligations imposed. For one thing, the enactment of this Bill could lead to a decrease in the willingness of health professionals to participate in later-gestation abortions due to a fear of criminal liability, which would have a disastrous effect on the availability of an area of health care that is already significantly under-serviced. The committee also expressed concern as to the likely effect of this Bill on patient-centred care and quality of care. Disappointingly, the committee declined to make any recommendations, 'noting the diverse and strong[ly] held views, and that this is a matter of conscience'.

Western Australian Abortion Law Reform

The most significant development to take place recently at the state level was the September 2023 reform of Western Australia's abortion laws. In a victory for reproductive rights, that state has finally brought its abortion law in line with the rest of the country. It has been twenty-five years since Western Australia last updated its abortion legislation. The 1998 arrest of two doctors created a climate of fear among the local medical profession, leading to a freezing of abortion services statewide, including lawful abortion services, and it precipitated the liberalisation of Western Australia's abortion laws. But after a quarter-century, the law had become outdated, particularly given that the rest of the country had enacted more progressive legislation.

The new law removes abortion from the criminal law realm and places it squarely within a health law framework, with the governing legislation being the *Public Health Act 2016*. It enhances legal access to abortion in a number of ways. For one thing, the new law states that the requirement for two medical practitioners to agree that the abortion is appropriate only applies after twenty-three weeks' gestation. This places Western Australia among the more progressive jurisdictions—third to the Australian Capital Territory, where there are no gestational limits to abortion on request, and Victoria, where abortion is available on request up to twenty-four weeks' gestation.

While very few abortions occur after twenty weeks in Australia, these are often the most devastating cases; for example, involving severe foetal abnormality. It is therefore essential that the law provides an avenue for patients to access abortions at all stages of gestation, with minimal barriers to this.

The new law also takes account of recent changes at the federal level, allowing nurse practitioners and endorsed midwives to prescribe medication for the conduct of a medical abortion. Given that most abortions occur at the early stages of gestation, this amendment should go a long way to enhancing access, especially in rural and remote areas. And while the amended legislation retains the right of health professionals with a conscientious objection to refuse to participate in an abortion, it brings Western Australia in line with other states by requiring a practitioner to disclose their objection and either transfer the patient's care or provide information on where the patient can access that care. Further, the duty to provide abortion care in an emergency supersedes any conscientious objection.

One of the oddities of the previous legislative provisions was the requirement for patients to receive counselling as part of the informed consent conditions. This prerequisite was out of step with all other Australian jurisdictions and created an unnecessary additional barrier for patients seeking care. Counselling should always be available for those who need or want it, but mandatory counselling is paternalistic and can result in delays, which is significant in the context of a procedure where the passage of time can make a big difference; for example, with respect to the availability of medical versus surgical abortion. The new law removes this requirement.

Finally, the new law removes the automatic requirement for parental involvement regarding minors under sixteen years of age. Now, in line with other areas of health law, a 'mature minor' may consent to an abortion without parental involvement. Medical practitioners are experienced at determining whether a minor is sufficiently mature and capable of making their own medical decisions.

THE WAY FORWARD

One of the reasons why it is important to frame abortion as a human rights issue, as this book has done, is because a human rights approach shifts power to the rights holder. If a person has a right to terminate a pregnancy, then they can demand that this right be protected and fulfilled. Of course, the question of who has the power, and who should have the power, is a constant undercurrent in conversations about how abortion should be regulated, and this question of power is gendered in nature.

The medical profession historically has been male-dominated, and the power differential between doctor and patient is exacerbated where the context involves a male doctor and a female patient. It is because of this context that I use gendered language in this final section of the book, noting my intention to be inclusive of all people who may need to access abortion services. The power dynamic I have described is further magnified where the health issue that a woman is experiencing is one involving reproduction—the circumstances of pregnancy, pregnancy termination and childbirth place women in uniquely vulnerable positions. Anyone who has been to the doctor for a routine gynaecological examination or who has experienced pregnancy or childbirth knows this to be an irrefutable fact.

Two disturbing accounts recently emerged from the United States that directly touch on this issue of power, gender and reproduction. The first was the class action against the Yale Fertility Centre in Connecticut, centred on a nurse who was a drug addict and stole the pain medication intended to be delivered to patients during egg retrieval. As a result, many patients underwent this procedure with little or no pain management, and their pleas for help were frequently minimised or ignored. The second involved the claims of hundreds of women that their obstetrician-gynaecologist at Columbia University in New York had sexually abused them—he continued his behaviour unrestrained for four decades before finally being convicted and sentenced in 2023.

Considering the power dynamics at play, how should abortion be regulated? I advocate a form of regulation that helps give back to women some of the power they have lost over years of having their health concerns, pain and suffering ignored, minimised, misdiagnosed or (at its worst) caused by the medical profession. For example, this is why I am arguing for the removal of gestational limits to abortion on request. But there are bigger questions here around whether there should be abortion-specific legislation at all, or whether abortion should simply be regulated within the general health law framework. I am in favour of the latter approach, as this would go some way to removing the exceptional status that has traditionally been accorded to abortion.

Finally, and sticking with the issue of gender and power, abortion is poorly funded and serviced in

Australia. I wonder if this would be the case if it was a form of health care predominantly required by men. I suspect not. So what is the way forward?

Relatively speaking, the laws in Australia are quite progressive, although jurisdictional differences remain. Abortion has been decriminalised nation-wide, and all states and territories have enacted safe access zones. But nonetheless I would like to see the removal of abortion-specific legislation and instead have abortion regulated within standard health care; at the very least, gestational limits for abortion on request should be removed. From a non-legal perspective, we need better training of medical practitioners; the normalisation of abortion and a corresponding reduction in stigma; and adequate publicly funded abortion care across urban, regional, rural and remote areas.

Several developments provide cause for optimism. The international human rights community has recognised the right to terminate a pregnancy as falling within the existing human rights paradigm, and its approach has influenced the liberalisation of abortion laws and the facilitation of enhanced access in various countries. In Australia, positive recent developments include easier access to medical abortion and the reform of Western Australia's abortion legislation.

However, I began this book by talking about the overturning of the 1973 decision of *Roe v Wade* in the United States in June 2022, removing the constitutional protection for abortion and paving the way for the banning or highly restrictive regulation of abortion in many American states. This is relevant not only because we should be concerned about violations of the fundamental human rights of all people, regardless of where they live, but also because of the growth of US-style anti-abortion advocacy here in Australia. This has been illustrated by the November 2022 Bill that homes in on the most rare and heartbreaking cases of later-gestation abortion, and which unjustifiably calls into question existing clinical practice so as to misrepresent the reality of what occurs. It uses a tragic scenario to drum up opposition to abortion.

We must remain vigilant and ensure that, in Australia, we continue to march towards reproductive justice, not away from it.

ACKNOWLEDGEMENTS

This book had a long build-up. I've been thinking and writing about abortion in Australia for over a decade, and I've been thinking about the international human rights approach for even longer. So I am grateful to Monash University Publishing for giving me the opportunity to consolidate my thoughts into a book, and to Paul Smitz for superb copyediting.

Thank you to the people who read through drafts, provided feedback and advised on 'readability': my parents, Adiva and Michael Sifris, and my husband, Michael Ross.

Thanks also to my co-authors over the years, especially Tania Penovic with whom I conducted a large, national empirical study on the need for, and impact of, safe access zones.

Thank you to Monash University's Castan Centre for Human Rights Law. I've been the centre's deputy director for a number of years, and that role has afforded me the opportunity to sink myself into the human rights realm, including reproductive rights.

Finally, thank you to the advocates, activists and warriors who have fought for, and continue to fight for, reproductive rights in Australia and beyond. May we reach a point where there are no more battles to fight and we have achieved full reproductive justice.

NOTES

1   Ronli Sifris, 'Now That *Roe v Wade* Has Been Overturned, What Are the Consequences?', *Monash Lens*, 27 June 2022.

2   World Health Organization, 'Fact Sheet: Abortions', 25 November 2021.

3   Alicia Ely Yamin and Agustina Ramón Michel, 'Engendering Democracy and Rights: The Legalization of Abortion in Argentina', in Mary Ziegler (ed.), *Research Handbook on International Abortion Law*, Edward Elgar, Northampton, MA, 2023, pp. 394, 411.

4   Olivia B Waxman, 'Ruth Bader Ginsburg Wishes This Case Had Legalized Abortion Instead of *Roe v Wade*', *Time*, 2 August 2018 (updated 24 June 2022).

5   Reva Siegel, 'Reasoning from the Body: A Historical Perspective on Abortion Regulation and Questions of Equal Protection', *Stanford Law Review*, vol. 44, 1992, p. 261.

6   See, for example, Catharine MacKinnon, 'The Male Ideology of Privacy: A Feminist Perspective on the Right to Abortion', *Radical America*, vol. 17, 1983, p. 23.

7   Manfred Nowak, *Report of the Special Rapporteur on Torture and other Cruel, Inhuman or Degrading Treatment or Punishment*, UN Doc A/HRC/7/3, 15 January 2008. p. 6.

8   Johanna B Fine et al., 'The Role of International Human Rights Norms in the Liberalization of Abortion Laws Globally', *Health and Human Rights Journal*, vol. 19, no. 1, 2017, p. 69.

9   Ibid., p. 71.

10 Ronli Sifris, 'Abortion and Human Rights: To What Extent Does Australian Law and Practice Facilitate a Woman's Right to Terminate a Pregnancy?', in Paula Gerber and Melissa Castan (eds), *Critical Perspectives on Human Rights Law in Australia*, Thomson Reuters, Melbourne, vol. 1, 2021, p. 251.

11 Lisa Teasdale, 'Confronting the Fear of Being "Caught": Discourses on Abortion in Western Australia', *University of New South Wales Law Journal*, vol. 22, no. 1, 1999, pp. 60, 63.

12 Ronli Sifris, 'Abortion in Australia: Law, Policy and the Advancement of Reproductive Rights', in Mary Ziegler (ed.), *Research Handbook on International Abortion Law*, Edward Elgar, Northampton, MA, 2023, pp. 124, 127–8.

13 Rebecca J Cook, 'Stigmatized Meanings of Criminal Abortion Law', in Rebecca J Cook, Joanna N Erdman and Bernard M Dickens (eds), *Abortion Law in Transnational Perspective: Cases and Controversies*, University of Pennsylvania Press, Philadelphia, 2014, p. 347.

14 Barbara Baird and Erica Millar, 'More than Stigma: Interrogating Counter Narratives of Abortion', *Sexualities*, vol. 22, 2019, p. 1110.

15 See World Health Organization, *Abortion Care Guideline*, 8 March 2022.

16 Donna Lu, 'These Women Were Told Their Babies Would Not Survive—but Catholic-Run Public Hospitals Refused to Provide Abortions', *The Guardian*, 6 September 2023.

17 *Clubb & Preston* (2019) 366 ALR 1, 75–6 [281] (footnotes omitted) per Nettle J, relying on the empirical research of Ronli Sifris and Tania Penovic that was referred to in submissions of the Castan Centre for Human Rights Law appearing as amicus curiae.

18 Interview with Philip Goldstone, medical director, Marie Stopes Australia (Ronli Sifris/Tania Penovic, 13 August 2019).

19 Ronli Sifris, 'Abortion in Australia: Law, Policy and the Advancement of Reproductive Rights', in Mary Ziegler (ed.), *Research Handbook on International Abortion Law*, Edward Elgar, Northampton, MA, 2023, pp. 124, 137–8.

20 Jo Wainer (ed.), *Lost: Illegal Abortion Stories*, Melbourne University Press, Carlton, 2006, pp. 124–5.

21 Ronli Sifris and Tania Penovic, 'Barriers to Abortion Access in Australia before and during the COVID-19 Pandemic', *Women's Studies International Forum*, vol. 86, 2021, p. 102470.

22 Hon Chuen Cheng and Caroline de Costa, 'Abortion Education in Medical Schools', *Australian and New Zealand Journal of Obstetrics and Gynaecology*, vol. 61, 2021, pp. 793, 796.

23 Hon Chuen Cheng et al., 'Views and Practices of Induced Abortion among Australian Fellows and Trainees of the Royal Australian and New Zealand College of Obstetricians and Gynaecologists: A Second Study', *Australian and New Zealand Journal of Obstetrics and Gynaecology*, vol. 60, 2020, p. 290.

24 Louise Anne Keogh et al., 'Conscientious Objection to Abortion, the Law and Its Implementation in Victoria, Australia: Perspectives of Abortion Service Providers', *BMC Medical Ethics*, vol. 20, no. 11, 2019.

25 Rachel Eddie, '"A Postcode Lottery": The 17 Areas with No Abortion Access in Victoria', *The Age*, 6 August 2023. It should be noted that, in November 2023, Victoria announced that three more hospitals in the state would offer surgical abortions. They are based in Melbourne's eastern and western suburbs and the Mornington Peninsula.

26 Interview with centre manager, Dr Marie Maroondah (Ronli Sifris/Tania Penovic, 26 October 2017).

27 At the time of writing, Queensland had just announced plans to allow nurses and midwives to facilitate a medical abortion. See Eden Gillespie, 'Queensland Introduces Australian-First Law to Allow Midwives and Nurses to Prescribe Abortion Pills', *The Guardian*, 30 November 2023.

(continued from previous page)

Andrew Jaspan & Lachlan Guselli *The Consultancy Conundrum: The Hollowing Out of the Public Sector*

Andrew Leigh *Fair Game: Lessons from Sport for a Fairer Society & a Stronger Economy*

Ian Lowe *Australia on the Brink: Avoiding Environmental Ruin*

John Lyons *Dateline Jerusalem: Journalism's Toughest Assignment*

Richard Marles *Tides that Bind: Australia in the Pacific*

Fiona McLeod *Easy Lies & Influence*

Michael Mintrom *Advancing Human Rights*

Louise Newman *Rape Culture*

Martin Parkinson *A Decade of Drift*

Isabelle Reinecke *Courting Power: Law, Democracy & the Public Interest in Australia*

Abul Rizvi *Population Shock*

Kevin Rudd *The Case for Courage*

Don Russell *Leadership*

Scott Ryan *Challenging Politics*

Kate Thwaites & Jenny Macklin *Enough Is Enough*

Simon Wilkie *The Digital Revolution: A Survival Guide*

Carla Wilshire *Time to Reboot: Feminism in the Algorithm Age*

Campbell Wilson *Living with AI*